Libraries Take Us Far

Libraries Take Us Far

a building block book

Lee Sullivan Hill

Carolrhoda Books, Inc./Minneapolis

For my husband, Gary, with love and Lifesavers candies—L. S. H.

For metric conversion, when you know the number of square feet, multiply by .09 to find the number of square meters. When you know the number of tons, multiply by .9 to find the number of metric tons.

The photographs in this book are reproduced through the courtesy of: Frye Gillan Molinaro Architects, Ltd., Chicago/© Stephan Graham Photography, front cover; © Scott Amundson Photography, back cover, p. 17; Sally Weigand, Images in Word & Picture, pp. 1, 7, 19; Phillips Swager Associates/© Michael Lyon, p. 2; Fanning Howey Associates Inc. Architects/Engineers/Consultants, and Emery Photography, pp. 6, 20; © Howard E. Ande, pp. 5, 13, 14, 25; © Pitkin Guides Ltd., p. 8; Library of Congress, p. 9; New Wave Photography, p. 10; Images International/© Joe Bellantoni, p. 11; Frye Gillan Molinaro Architects, Ltd., Chicago/© George Lambros Photography, p. 12; Boston Public Library/Michael Maloney, p. 15; Images International/© Charlie Riedel, p. 16; Images International/© Erwin C. "Bud" Nielsen, p. 18; © Robert Perron, pp. 21, 28; © Stewart Cohen/Tony Stone Images, Inc., p. 22; © Robert E. Daemmrich/Tony Stone Images, Inc., p. 23; © Mitch Kezar/Tony Stone Images, Inc., p. 24; © Steven Ferry, p. 26; © James J. Hill Reference Library, p. 27; Frye Gillan Molinaro Architects, Ltd., Chicago, p. 29.

Carolrhoda Books, Inc., c/o The Lerner Publishing Group
241 First Avenue North, Minneapolis, Minnesota, U.S.A. 55401

Website address: www.lernerbooks.com

Library of Congress Cataloging-in-Publication Data

Hill, Lee Sullivan, 1958–
    Libraries take us far / Lee Sullivan Hill.
      p. cm. — (A building block book)
    Summary: Surveys all kinds of libraries, from a monastery library full of handmade books to a school media center to a bookmobile.
      ISBN 1-57505-072-2
      1. Libraries—Juvenile literature. 2. Libraries—United States—Juvenile literature.
    [1. Libraries.] I. Title. II. Series: Hill, Lee Sullivan, 1958– Building block book.
    Z665.5.H56   1998
    027—dc21   97–16234

Manufactured in the United States of America
1 2 3 4 5 6 SP 03 02 01 00 99 98

Libraries are close to home. But they can take you far away. All you need is a library card to start you on your way.

Your school library is right down the hall.
Is it called the learning center or the media center
or simply the library? Whatever you call it,
you'll find shelves and shelves of books there.

In the Middle Ages, books were rare. Each was made by hand. Silver and gold and beautiful colors sparkled from the pages. Kings and scholars kept these treasures locked up in private libraries.

In some libraries, books were even chained to the shelves!

The invention of the printing press changed libraries. In the 1450s, Johann Gutenberg fit small metal letters into a press. He spread ink on the letters and could print pages by the hundreds. Printers made books by the thousands. Rich people built private libraries to hold their collections.

Books became more common, but they still cost a lot. Benjamin Franklin had an idea. Why not share the cost? Ben and some friends started the Library Company of Philadelphia in 1731. People paid to join. With this money, the library bought books for members to share.

The first free libraries opened in the 1800s. One was in Salisbury, Connecticut. Caleb Bingham loved to read when he was a boy. But he could never find enough books in Salisbury.

After Caleb grew up and moved away, he sent more than one hundred books to his hometown. It was the start of a free library for Salisbury.

Many libraries began with gifts. As a boy, Andrew Carnegie worked long hours in a mill. He had no time for school. He learned by reading books. After he became rich, he wanted to give away some of his money. His gifts helped many towns build libraries.

People still need new libraries. Workers dug this big hole in Schaumburg, Illinois. Soon, a new library will stand here. People can't wait until it opens. The library will have space for books, magazines, videos, and computers.

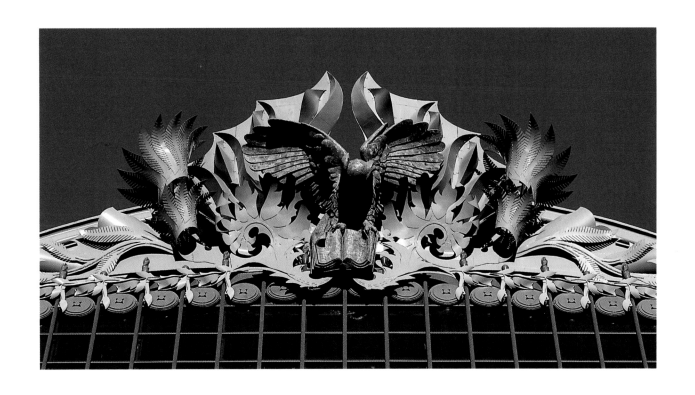

The city of Chicago opened the Harold Washington Library Center in 1991. It holds almost two *million* books! Huge owls perch like gargoyles at the rooftop. Are they there to guard the books?

Big cities have big libraries. Wide stone steps lead to the entrance of the Boston Public Library. Giant-sized arches frame the doors. But don't worry. The books inside fit right in your hands.

Not all libraries are huge. Some find space for their books in a small storefront.

Others load their books in a van. Bookmobiles are libraries on wheels. They travel from place to place. (Spending time in a bookmobile might *really* take you far!)

On wheels or in a building, all libraries
hold books. Some also have photos and letters
and papers from famous people. Research
libraries help people study the past and plan
for the future.

University libraries give students room to work and think. Peek out from the balcony at tables and chairs and glowing lamps. Around the corner, books of stories, books of facts, fill every cranny, left and right.

Take a trip to a library. What do you hear?
People ask questions. Pages turn. Computers
whir. Quiet sounds fill up the space.

Go to the children's room at a public library. If it's story hour, listen to the librarian read aloud. You might hear children singing or babies crying. It gets loud in there!

Libraries have quiet places, too. Look past the
rows of shelves. Are students bent over books,
studying for a test?

All libraries help you find answers to questions. Who lives in the rain forest? What did pioneers eat? When do spiders sleep? You can find these facts and more. Ask a librarian.

When you grow up, you could become a
librarian and learn where to find answers.

You could help build
new libraries for children
everywhere. Or you
could go to your library
and check out a book and
a movie.

But don't wait until you grow up. Go to the
library now. Read a new book. Find out about
your favorite animal.

Click on the computer. Search for facts about
a place you've never seen.

Libraries help us learn and wonder. They let
us travel with the magic of words.

Libraries take us far.

A Photo Index to the Libraries in This Book

Cover This building may look like a space station, but it's actually a library in Portage, Michigan.

Page 1 Built in 1890, the Fisher Fine Arts Library at the University of Pennsylvania in Philadelphia is one of several libraries on the university campus.

Page 2 Builders of this library in Euless, Texas, closed off some of the rooms and left them unfinished. Bookshelves, carpets, and ceilings will be added later when the library needs more room.

Page 5 A family gave their house to the townspeople of Wyandotte, Michigan, in 1942 to use as a library. In the children's room, one of the house's old tubs has been turned into a reading nook!

Page 6 Woodbrook Elementary School in Carmel, Indiana, calls this space a media center. The center has lots of computers in addition to shelves of books.

Page 7 The main library at Oxford University in England was founded in the 1300s and was added onto many times. It was named the Bodleian Library in 1604 to honor Sir Thomas Bodley, who gave books and support to the library.

Page 8 The library at Hereford Cathedral in England is called a chained library. These days, librarians use modern security systems to keep track of books. (Some librarians probably wish they still had chains!)

Page 9 An original copy of the Gutenberg Bible is at the Library of Congress in Washington, D.C. Visit the library's Website at www.loc.gov to find out what other treasures are at the largest library in the world.

Page 10 Ben Franklin's collection of books from the 1700s has turned into a research library that holds more than 500,000 rare books, manuscripts, and periodicals. The Library Company of Philadelphia moved to this building on Locust Street in 1965.

 **Page 11** Scoville Memorial Library was built in 1895. Carved oak trim and a huge fireplace make the inside look like a castle. The books that Caleb Bingham donated in 1803 are on display in a special collection.

 **Page 12** Could this library in Edwardsville, Illinois, be a gift from Andrew Carnegie? The building looks brand new, yet Carnegie died in 1919. The answer is yes and no. The original library, built in 1906, *was* Carnegie's gift. This addition was finished in 1990.

 **Page 13** The Schaumburg Township District is the largest library system in Illinois, aside from that of Chicago. The new building will have 160,000 square feet of space. That's almost as big as four football fields put together.

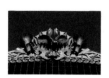 **Page 14** The Harold Washington Library Center is in downtown Chicago. The owls and trim at the rooftop are cast aluminum, painted green to look like weathered copper. Each bird weighs almost four tons.

 **Page 15** Boston Public Library was one of the first free city libraries. It was founded in 1854 and was moved into the McKim Building in 1895. Architect Charles Follen McKim wanted the building to look like a beautiful Italian palace.

 **Page 16** The Grainfield City Library fills all three rooms in a small building. It has books and magazines for everyone in this Kansas farming town of 360 people.

 **Page 17** The Minneapolis Public Library bookmobile stops at apartment houses, day care centers, and community centers. Anyone with a library card can borrow a book and return it when the bookmobile makes its rounds again.

 **Page 18** The Lyndon B. Johnson Library is a research library at the University of Texas in Austin. It holds the papers and letters of Lyndon Baines Johnson, the 36th president of the United States.

Page 19 Does this picture remind you of the picture on page one? This is another view of the reading room in the Fisher Fine Arts Library at the University of Pennsylvania.

Page 20 Children check out books at Twin Valley South. It's in West Alexandria, Ohio.

Page 21 Everyone's getting ready for story hour in the children's room of the Thomaston, Connecticut, public library. It sure looks noisy!

Page 22 Quiet areas in libraries allow college students to get ready for tests.

Page 23 A student librarian is helping this boy find the book he needs. What do you look for when you go to the library?

Page 24 A librarian helps a student in the reference section of a college library. The two are surrounded by atlases, dictionaries, globes, and encyclopedias, from A to Z.

Page 25 This carpenter is placing concrete wall forms for a library basement. By the time the building is finished, hundreds of skilled workers will have helped in its construction.

Page 26 Libraries such as the New Port Richey Public Library in Florida hold *so many* good books. Do you have a favorite?

Page 27 The computers at the James J. Hill Reference Library in Saint Paul, Minnesota, are always busy. Computers help people find facts quickly, on library databases or on the Internet.

Page 28 Children soak up the magic of words on a summer day in Connecticut. Killingworth Library has an outdoor spot for story hour that is also used as a stage.

Page 29 Rows of steel columns, topped with triangles, draw visitors into the Midlothian, Illinois, public library.

WITHDRAWN